"Prepare to ri
the author, moving on a riptide of forgetting and con-
fusion, down into the murky depths of nothingness, to
suddenly emerge on the other side of awareness with
a gasp, ready to fill the next blank page with whatever
comes next."

    —HEIDI BARR, author of *Woodland Manitou*

"As a nurse, I'm moved by this glimpse into a patient's
experience; everyone caring for people with traumatic
brain injury should read it. As I writer, I marvel at Naw-
rocki's skill and elegance portraying the grief and grace,
the mystery and the miraculousness, and yes, the hope
and humor in waking up."

    —IRIS GRAVILLE, author of
Hiking Naked: A Quaker Woman's Search for Balance

"Nawrocki's experience is nothing short of a shamanic
journey, a rite of passage, in which she emerges with pro-
found insights—insights that come not from her mem-
ories but from the emptiness of this forgotten time."

    —THEODORE RICHARDS,
author of *The Great Re-Imagining*

The Comet's Tail

The Comet's Tail

A Memoir of No Memory

Amy Nawrocki

THE LITTLE BOUND BOOKS ESSAY SERIES

Personal. Poignant. Powerful.

The author has tried to recreate events, locales and
conversations from her memories of them. In order to
maintain their anonymity in some instances she has changed
the names of individuals and places, she may have changed
some identifying characteristics and details such as physical
properties, occupations and places of residence.

Published in 2018 • Little Bound Books
Imprint of Homebound Publications
Front Cover Image © by EkaterinaP | Shutterstock.com
Cover and Interior Designed • Leslie M. Browning
ISBN • 978-1-947003-61-3
First Edition Trade Paperback

10 9 8 7 6 5 4 3 2 1

Homebound Publications is committed to ecological
stewardship. We greatly value the natural environment and
invest in environmental conservation. Our books are printed
on paper with chain of custody certification from the Forest
Stewardship Council, Sustainable Forestry Initiative, and the
Program for the Endorsement of Forest Certification.

For my family
Save the pieces

These are the things I do remember: I do remember driving home on lightless highways from my summer job in New Haven, windows half-rolled, thick June air blowing around me. I do remember emptying my bank account to buy a fish tank for fish that died. I remember falling asleep to James Brown and recordings of electrical thunderstorms. I remember my bedroom—there were three white walls and one red one. The bed's brass frame probably needed polishing as it always did. I remember not feeling like myself, and something about yelling, and I remember calling for friends from work. I think I remember Dad rattling into my room: "What's wrong?" I do not remember dread or panic. I do not remember seizures, quivering like a wind-up toy let loose from its coil. I do not remember the tubes, the tests, or the icy cold of space. I do not remember losing six months of my life.

How can I write a memoir about events for which I have no memory? As a trial transcript? A lab report? An academic's footnoted research? In short, it is the story of a coma, of an illness lasting nearly six months. The setting is easy to establish: the summer after my freshman year of college. A lens zooms into pins on a map—a house in Sandy Hook and three hospitals, each with names and purpose, wood and stone, concrete and steel. Run a string between the pins and a lazy lasso takes shape. The character is a nineteen-year-old girl who can't speak. There is action, and there is conflict. Hospital doors slip into their grooves without effort. A body thrashes, eyes open and close, hands fold in prayer. Needles penetrate skin, electrodes trace monotony and chart the spiked parabola of fever. No one knows what to do. The lasso, held by others, wants to loop me back into the world, but I can't catch it.

In the retelling, I could start with infection. I could start with screaming. I could work backward from a slice of cranberry orange bread, tasted many months later and cataloged in unsettled penmanship. Or maybe I could re-imagine a single haircut, my first plane ride, a walk home from the bus stop, or any of the moments when an inner monologue secretly records that little voice inside that says, *I am me.* There are probably a thousand such moments when skin and soul understand each other, moments of recognition that this body, this outward gaze, this being is the one I have always had.

But point of view is tricky. Is this *my* story? The protagonist's perspective, inevitably, is passive. Everything happened *to* me. There is nothing to embellish—I got sick, I fell into a deep sleep, I woke up. No fairytale.

I can't remember a time when I didn't live in my head, and I can't remember a time when I felt totally comfortable in my body. Throughout high school in suburban Connecticut, I earned good grades and built close ties with a small group of girls, preferring small circles to parties or popularity. Over time, I gained self-esteem by relying on literature, friendships, and Weight Watchers. In the traumatic months when my mother was sick, and even after she died, I could tap into strength, not deterioration. I liked myself and looked forward to Sarah Lawrence College.

When I try to reconstruct that year, I picture that eighteen-year-old college student who loved books, '80s pop, and comfortable shoes. Like most freshmen, I thought I would figure things out along the way. My college ID card captured the first day on campus, and I look like a lost puppy trying to be cool. My hair was short, earrings were long; I wore an olive tank top under a sweater with loose stitching that breathed more than I did. In those first months, I played along, bumming cigarettes at parties, carrying my dorm key around on a silk string, sharing my roommate's computer to type papers. The semester progressed to autumn routines and shades of rain, classroom roundtables, and conference papers. Derek Walcott and Dostoevsky, salt bagels with cream cheese and tomato. Frozen yogurt and poems. I had a poster of John Lennon above my bed, a cactus named Dickey—overwatered and brown by winter— and the dictionary dog-eared to the list of presidents I memorized in the tangle of insomnia. I also kept a notebook with scribbles and streamlined day-to-day thoughts. As it turns out, these pages provide back-story, maybe even understory, for what would come.

> 24 February: Today I am without sky. Diagnosis: I have fear. Chronologically, I'm due for a mood swing anytime soon.

The journal—a creative workspace suggested by my poetry teacher—began sometime in autumn after the habits of classes had settled into shape. There were two notebooks, I'm sure of it, but only the second survived. On the red cover of the university five-subject notebook, two hundred college-ruled sheets measuring 9.5 by 6 inches, I centered a pen-drawn flower, a rudimentary dove, and an abstract doodle captioned "man walking dog." Inside, I wrote rambling passages about my course readings, about procrastinating, about bored nights at the campus coffee house. There were only a few passages about friends and teachers, fewer about physical land-scapes and campus maps. Quirky, automatic writings centered on such things as the migratory patterns of zebras, delinquent toe hairs, daisies, and seafoam. Mostly, I worked through whatever small traumas came up, plotting my way through the most ordinary case of first-year blues. The semesters fused: One entry in December chronicled the end of the first term and the train ride home for Christmas. Over break, the new year came without much of comment; back on campus, I turned nineteen.

> 18 February: I suppose in the long run I'll have to give back all the childhoods I stole, all the Lincoln logs [and] believability.

For workshops, I wrote what I thought epitomized the artistry of a "real" poet, cataloging emotions that could not be articulated except in metaphor. The free-writes kept me afloat; they were sometimes witty, often melancholy, more often false bravado:

02 March: I am not a delicate flower. I am not the likeness of a leopardess, I am the energy of a tidal wave. I am the catastrophe of a raindrop. I am an orchid, I am a lily. I am a life and death without a mask. I am a fork and a forklift. I am rubbish of apple seeds. I am mother, I am earth, and when I speak, I call up windlessness and ask its name.

As the second semester continued, the journals captured a voice that was tired, working hard, and trying to fit in. Long nights writing and longer nights not sleeping. Solitude did not seem as fun as it was when I played on my own in the back yard, making up stories on the long way home from the bus stop. My internal monologue never ceased. I wanted to rest, not from school necessarily, or family, or work, but from thinking *all the time*. Transcribing these thoughts was not a restful act, and as pages went on, the ideas became more and more coded and mysterious. I seemed to fixate on my physical mind, making uncanny allusions.

09 March: I found boredom to be sleepless under a rock of drug induced comatose crustaceans. This, I'm sure is also the place where the meaning of life finds nutrients but alas, once comatose always comatose . . . When I have children I'm having them in my brain.

I can't recall writing any one day's entry. Sometimes I lay on my bed; sometimes I sat in the library. I remember poetry was on the first floor, inhabiting Dewey's decimals between 811 and 812. Reserve reading was in the basement, where the microfiche held all the old memories twisted on cellulose roles and projected like ghosts onto now-ancient machines. The moments, like all things in the past, have vanished like clouds blown by a breeze. Even so, I can hear myself in the voice of that girl.

15 April: And the whole world ended before I was ready, before I could catch a pin drop, before I could plant a fruit tree of experience (memory) in the top soil . . . Five past eleven on a Tuesday . . . Atom splitting headaches refusing to accept the Copernican model of the

universe. Palm strike to the face. . . I'm tired of
this now that ebb tides the flow. Jump to my
death, said the mailman.

As buds bloomed on campus, I was scrambling to
finish a term paper about the Cold War, sketching
a design for a tattoo, leaving my army-store canvas
coat in the closet, and planning my transfer escape.
Maybe the realization that college wasn't the sanc-
tuary I expected created anxiety, but my writing
became more desperate, and more literally cerebral.
Even so, I don't remember unbearable migraines or
needing to visit the health center for physical pain.
Instead, I wished the thought-cycles would end.
When I visited a counselor, he told me I had to let
myself off the hook of inadequacy.

21 April: Sometimes I wonder if it's my own
life I'm remembering. Sometimes I wonder if
it's my own life I've been living. Sometimes I
wonder if my dreams and my reality will merge
. . . Sometimes I wonder if I am getting an ulcer
. . . Sometimes I wonder if all this wondering
isn't detrimental to my mental health. Like

now for instance, my stomach is in turmoil. It's about time it caught up with my head.

These descriptions of maladies and neurons, comas and catastrophes signaled a very rational concept: writing turns ideas into concrete letters on the page. If I identified with a brain that was close to overload, it was because my thoughts needed release. The mind, where memory resides, seemed an obvious symbol at the time.

28 April: My mind is thick with clutter and panic. I feel ill. I feel faint. I feel like a million bucks, or not. . . I am a nightingale and my voice is midnight. Soft and low. Momentum strong, like a cat, feline and shadowy. What is blue? . . . Shit said the dog. Dancing with mahogany, losing the ozone, fearing death, hoping for appendicitis. Ok, stop procrastinating, Time to do some work. Time to fall into a pit and bury myself. "She died," said my tombstone, "she lived," said my wings.

A detective must always work backward, and only in retrospect do these writings suggest that a corridor exists between the unconscious and the conscious, through whatever passageway the body will allow. Who knows how much of ourselves we really hear, even within an echoing mind?

> 30 April: So you sold your gall bladder to go to the Spinal Tap concert. And not to mention the brain scan . . . My deepest fear is that I'll really like the pain . . . Beached whales and a herd of goats charging off the edge of a cliff. One 4th of a snowflake. One quarter of my life I've spent in the cold forming frost melting and turning to water. I am unlike any other. A snow flower, unique.

Were these prophecies and premonitions? Intuition? Cryptograms needing code-breakers? Perhaps mention of brain scans and spinal taps were completely coincidental. Perhaps, like other symbols (goats, snowflakes, mountains) these were just ramblings. But I cannot deny their relevance because two months later I would face a life-threatening brain fever.

05 May: My brain aches, my spirit is crusted
. . . The lameness of life is heavy . . . I am earth.
I am a moon drop. I must quit this earth and
raise sheep in Iowa. Wait, I am Iowa. Sleep my
woolen ones, sleep.

However abstract they are, meandering thoughts do
not cause brain fever in a physical, literal sense. The
mind keeps unconscious tabs on its body. Aches and
pain find their outlets far from a source; viruses can
linger. But if that was the case, then I cannot take
credit for these small glimpses of creativity that came
as I wrote down ideas. If the fever existed that far
back, then I am a sick nineteen-year-old with hallu-
cinations, not a poet splitting atoms with words. If
that's the story, then it's a witchdoctor I need, not a
neurologist.

08 May Friday night: I opened the solar panel
in my head and re-al (interesting)-ized {real-
ized} that the sun's radiation had caused my
brain cells to mutate—hence my mania. The
verdict is in—I have decided against reality.
I have chosen to scorn this life and take my

rightful place on Mount Olympus as a fly . . .
In my dreams when I try to run I feel shack-
led unfairly by gravity. Like trying to run from
a magnet . . . emphasizing the question mark,
creasing your eyebrows, sneering your lips,
wishing secretly that I would die already . . .
And as closure is embodied in a paper clip, I
too am twisted and wired to fasten.

The journal does not clearly pinpoint the last few
days on campus. May 11th, I prose out a poem about
jackals and earthworms, about time "boxed and elec-
tric" sagging into my arms. "Later," I wrote, "I would
board the train back to Connecticut, back to the lace
and emptiness of world." I packed up the dorm room
soon after and went home, unsure about where I
would be when fall classes started again. Back in my
childhood bedroom, the entries I wrote were narrow
and brusque, but I don't remember writing them out
of confusion, anticipation, or even fear. I was feel-
ing my way out of college life and into the interim
summer break.

22 May: Said the man to the woman: Forget me, I have nothing to give. I am nothing. Forgive me, said the woman because I will forget you . . . To end or not to end that is the question. END. But this is only the beginning. Haven for the sick, end.

23 May: FUCK THE WORLD, she said, blazing like a cross, blaze motherfucker, blaze, end.

28 May: And the waltz burned in fainted melody. Walk with me, dance of sweet remembrance. People are stupid. end.

This is the last entry in the journal, seven days before my memory would go to sleep. How accurate is a written record, even when it registers, day by day, the progress of what was really happening? The diarist's aim is not record keeping, and the poet's aim is to mold these recollections into something else. In those entries, I was saying goodbye—goodbye to the first year of college, goodbye to the dorm room, to the few friends I had made, to the claustrophobia of it all. Without realizing it, I also said goodbye to the body, brain, and inner-self that I had known for nineteen years. I was embarking on a new, horrific journey.

I would find the journal and that old self again, but it would be a long, strange while before I did. Across an open sky, the comet's tail disappears into dust. We may read in the particles proof of existence.

All that I know of the next six months has been pieced in retrospect. But this uncertainty is gentle, like a sweater over open shoulders. It warms me just enough in the blank chill of no memory. There are witnesses and records, and these must fill in the empty journal pages of the summer. Setting serves plot, even if the point of view shifts. When others begin scripts of their own, even if their records are more objective, these too are imperfect.

Hospitals are easy to conjure, and I can transfer actual memories from past visits to Danbury's Hospital's ICU because this is where my mother's cancer was diagnosed. In my mind's eye, I can see the position of the nurses' station, the theatre of curtains, doors that opened when you stepped toward them. A jar of purple liquid. Whether the blood sample belonged to mom or if it existed at all, my gaze tunnels onto something that made me search my tenth-grade vocabulary—*malignant*. That night, as we drove home in the Chevy Suburban, I watched a solid white star follow me home. When I pointed it out to my sister Shelly, she told me it was just a satellite. A year later, we sat in another hospital room, one with a centered desk, diplomas hanging on the wall. The doctor told us that she wouldn't live more than a couple weeks. He looked like all doctors: a tie, parted hair, stethoscope, and pocket pen. That was Saturday. She died early Monday, but not in the hospital where I would lay unconscious two and a half years later. She died at home surrounded by her own stenciled walls. I slept that night on the couch three rooms away. Those rooms I do remember.

The beginning weeks of the summer included a short trip to Cape Cod with my friend Sarah and a canvassing job with Greenpeace. Though spring was not yet over, I remember heat. I remember driving the used Datsun to New Haven and meeting a few new faces that I wouldn't know long enough to remember by name or appearance. My brothers remember screams in the middle of the night. There was a restless a car ride and an emergency room that I do not remember.

My siblings' recollections and some surviving documents establish the chronology, though pooling between them creates more mysteries. My father's experiences were haphazardly transcribed in shorthand by attending physicians. On June 3rd or 4th, I didn't feel well, complaining to Dad of headaches and a stiff neck, took lots of Tylenol. He said I had been acting erratically, argumentative and aggressive, sleeping little but not appearing sleepy. It's not clear how long I acted that way.

These days are difficult to reshape, compressed by so many years, my brothers' youth, and my sister's absence. Dad never talked much about it. My youngest brother Erick remembered everything in fragments. As a thirteen-year-old, his room was across the hall from mine, and he heard one chilling outburst. Kris,

15, can't recall the timeline exactly, but thought I was having a mental breakdown. According to Michael, who was the closest to me in age, Dad woke him up in the middle of the night. When he got up, I was in the kitchen, babbling incoherently. Dad drove me to the emergency room sometime around 3 a.m. An initial spinal tap showed nothing; at least that's what the notes say. By the time we came home, Michael had missed his alarm but left for school after telling Dad to take the day off. What I do remember from that day is vague: I can see the bathroom sink and remember standing there staring at a box of suppositories. As I became more and more disoriented, Dad drove me back to the emergency room. My neighbor held my seizing body from the back seat. I was admitted to Danbury Hospital on June 10th, apparently transferred on the 18th, though Shelly, away on a college internship in D.C., thought I was "whisked away to Yale" almost immediately.

Like my college journal, the medical records put dates to the story but more importantly describe the plot. The "history" and "progress notes" are a curious narrative of repetition and imposed structure. These early Xeroxed pages of hand written notes document the interpretations of a dozen different doctors. The monologues are dated and time stamped. Initials are scribbled in the margins. Most begin with the same practiced announcement: 19-year-old female, encephalitis of unknown origin, admitted for further diagnostic evaluation. Some give more details, "writes poetry," or "no travel outside of northeast," or "mother died of cancer 3 yrs. ago." "Father very anxious and concerned . . . continues to offer support." One resident politely admits that he or she was "asked to monitor this 19-year-old female college student;" another seems genuinely appreciative for the consultation request.

Doctors write with trained objectivity, which is necessary and correct. At least eleven people tell the story of Amy on June 18th when I arrive in "soft restraints." None of them knew me, and yet there is a curious honesty in their words. Some of them must have been interns on rotation, trying to establish themselves as competent and capable in the eyes of their peers and superiors. Most of them were probably only a few years older than I was. As trainees and onlookers, they're practicing the language of medicine, but their vocabulary does not match the typed reports—full of vague syntax and multisyllabic words—that come later. The specialists would take over, wave their expertise like wands, consider the heft of their magic instead of the consequences of their spells.

More formal reports are submitted from dermatology, neurophysiology, cytopathology, anatomic pathology. Multiple chest films are ordered. MRIs are deciphered; electroencephalograms chart my catatonic brain waves with "fast paper speed asymmetry" and single inked lines drawn by machine fingers on graph paper. Now, all these years later, I try to piece them together, and the narrative I come up with is equally sterile and mysterious. I must become a reporter, typing notes, organizing dates, and deciphering sign-offs. Between the lines of these copies is white space and reluctance. I tease out the details.

The patient is a nineteen-year-old female who does not respond to stimuli. She does not know a tube has been inserted into her trachea nor that she is being fed through her nose. She is writhing, retching, drooling. The eyes are roving; the arms are posturing. The body has rashes, bruises, and lesions. There is a partially collapsed lung and fever spikes that arch her back and shake her limbs. She is given Valpronic Acid, Dilantin, Thorazine, Ativan, Versed, Heparin, Pepcid, Carafate, and Vecuronium. She is in a vegetative state.

I'm looking at someone else's records. The coma girl has detached herself from me. I have to dream her up or rely on what others saw, eye witnesses who had to detach themselves in a different way.

Early feedback offered nothing to indicate what might be causing the varied and disturbing symptoms. Nothing viral, bacterial, or poisonous was found. My brother Michael thought I was on drugs; maybe I had dropped acid at work. There was the tattoo that I hadn't told anyone about. Bad needles? Stress-induced personality changes of a typical college student? With no explanations, the first option was the neuro-psych ward. Once when Michael and Kris visited, the nurses told them I was too agitated to see them. Security was tight, and Michael described, "not quite padded walls," but intense. High doses of medication kept me still, though my body continued to seize and stiffen erratically. A ventilator was inserted. CAT scans and MRIs and angioplasty showed little, but a third blood test revealed an elevated white blood count, pointing to something attacking the brain. Shelly remembered getting frantic phone calls from Dad, who seemed impatient and distracted when she asked to hear the word again— encephalitis—having no context for this disease's name. Hypotheses arose about whether it was "Triple E," Eastern Equine Encephalitis, or Lyme, but causes or origins were never settled on definitively. Shelly remembered someone calling our house that summer asking for me. Apparently, whoever was on the line was interested in conducting a study about "cat scratch fever," one of the potential causes which were thrown around early on. One doctor scribbled a note mentioning that we had a cat at home.

While nodes pinched skin, "occasional choreiform movements" noted during EEG and "continuous chewing" signaled a disconnect between brain and body. I could not follow commands and gave no response to verbal clues. In various reports, doctors recognized no decisive movement of arms, but at other times spontaneous, aimless movement. At least once, I swung my legs over the railing "purposefully," but they were "unable to reliably assess toes because of thrashing." A multi-sequence MRI on July 10, noted "one-month history of profound coma." This was how the story went through the summer: mental silence against limbs that spoke in spasms. Charts seemed to indicate that there was little connection between the two.

My father, bewildered and frightened, could not fathom what was happening to his daughter. Somehow, he had the wherewithal to tell my uncles and aunts where to park when then got to downtown New Haven. Without direct answers from physicians, he contacted my cousin Nancy, herself a doctor. She flew from California to help my father deal with confused and confusing experts. When she arrived, she found me in the intensive care unit at Yale New Haven Hospital, contorting grotesquely in what were probably continuing seizures. Doctors asked dad to sign a release. Having run out of solutions, they wanted to do an open brain biopsy the next morning and remove a slice of my frontal lobes about the size of a quarter.

Nancy remembered the neurologist explaining that it was "no big deal." She told them, "Amy was a poet before she got sick, and when she gets better, I think she might need that piece of frontal lobe." The neurologist shot back with a look of "bewilderment . . . condescension . . . pity." As she saw it, their job had little to do with finding me lost in "autonomic storms," breathing tubes and bite sticks, IVs dripping with tranquilizers. Their approach was objective and sterile. But now, my family's job would shift from fearful watchers to patient caregivers. Uncle Dana and Aunt Diana alternated their weekends between New Haven and Maine, where my cousin was at music camp. My friends came regularly. They moved closer to my bed, brought my things from home. Kara helped Nancy search through my journals and poems and recreate the weeks leading up to the crisis. Sian made a mix-tape titled "Get Your Butt Out in the Sun," playing "Back to Life" over and over. She and Amanda had to tone down their selections while in the hospital room but everyone spoke in soft voices directly into my ears. Whispers about rivers and willow trees, images of beauty, resilience, and strength. Poetry and music, voices I needed to remember. Hands that loved me touched my head to quell the fevers.

Doctors were looking for immediate responses, but Nancy found that I could perform small movements after a delay. She worked to get me to move my fingers, turn my head, react to voices, and use my own. About eleven o'clock one night, she asked me to stick out my tongue and move my fingers as a first-year resident came through on rounds. He shook my hand, stiff and uncooperative, and said, "not much to go on." When I curled into a ball, he left, indicating to the nurses that I "needed more drugs." Nancy and the night nurses turned to look at me. "Slowly, but surely," she said, "with an eerie persistence," I stuck out my tongue. It took her "another half hour to convince [me] to put it back in [my] mouth."

Whatever memories I might have formed may have been blocked by a cocktail of drugs that aimed to calm my limbs and measure whatever still hung in the understory of consciousness. In all of this, the conflicts between one doctor's approach and another's inevitably paralleled the unknowable space between what the body needed and what its spirit wanted. But a point of view shift doesn't mean the story is forged; an unreliable narrator needs an arc to follow. I trust my cousin's intuitions, my father's devotion, my friends' commitment to remember me as I had been and to urge me back to myself. It is not false modesty which detaches me now from the notion of a heroic return from unconsciousness. I want to be the girl who rebelliously poked her tongue out and stuck her middle finger up at doctors who saw only surfaces. But I can't remember her, and without that, I have no agency to see what I did as miraculous. I want the music of the spheres, but all I have is space dust.

On subsequent days in August, I was observed for ten hours of electroencephalography, given Valproic Acid and Tegretol. "Moderate deltas with occasional theta activity. Not responsive to light." But no seizures. Eye deviations and "right side jerking." On

August 25th "patient [was] turning toward therapist and smiling" but at that time, there were still delayed responses to following simple commands like raising my arm. Eyelids fluttered, lips moved, but no speech. "She follows simple verbal and motion commands and performs simple tasks after having hand-over-hand initiation." Soon, I could comb my hair and brush my teeth if someone started me. After these signs of small progress, the end of August comes, only slight advances but no real improvements.

I toggle between the subjectivity of other people's memories and the objectivity of chest x-rays and EEGs. If I returned from my space travel enough to be taken off a ventilator as Nancy recalled, why did the tracheostomy tube still warrant concern through July and August? When are the feeding tubes inserted? Why did subsequent reports focus on the minutia of long term debilitation? Why didn't I wake up? Each transcription seemed a dialogue with a previous test. These reports, too, challenge my notion that repetition aids memory. Like a chanted mantra, "impression: no significant change," signed off above a scribbled signature. Clinical follow-ups, summaries, diagnostic consolations. Fevers without origin, a partially collapsed lung. Catheters were named. Radiographs ordered. The location of the left subclavian feeding tube was in "good location" and unchanged.

> Over the approximate 3-month hospital course, the patient eventually slowly progressed and was taking [sic] completely off sedating medications . . . and the patient became more and more alert, began tracking, began to have more interactive periods. However, remained nonverbal and mostly did not follow commands.

School was starting soon. Shelly needed to finish her senior year of college. Michael returned to captain the high school football team to the state championship. Kris entered his junior year, Erick became a freshman. My friends all went back for their sophomore years at college. Back in session as a middle school guidance counselor, Dad still visited me every day after work.

According to Uncle Dana, sometime around Labor Day, my family was called for a conference with the doctors. They admitted again that they were at a loss as to what to do. Dana remembers one of them said, "What I am about to propose will literally either kill her or cure her. We have exhausted all other options. We want your permission to induce a deeper coma in the hope that Mother Nature will do what we cannot." After praying, the consensus was to go ahead. A length of time was mentioned, but Dana does not remember how long the deep coma lasted. One report says over a week, summarizing that under twenty-four-hour monitoring EEGs revealed "moderate to severe bilateral slowing but no epileptiform activity or interictal activity was discovered."

We all have simple language that gives away *sleep* in favor of *hibernation*—the earthly, animalistic time travel, hunkering down in a warm cave. We all have wished to dream ourselves beyond the stratosphere, to rocket past the Oort cloud and hitch a ride on a revolving arm of the galaxy. We all have wanted to get away, for a day, a night, a weekend, a season in some other space. "In my sleeplessness," I wrote months before the summer of no memory, "I hear an opera." I would love to take that imagined song and create a symphony of hyperconsciousness. I want to think of the summer as a time when I listened to deep odes that only I could hear, hiding in the thin silk of my own chrysalis. I want to touch with kinesthetic memory the letters written by fifth graders in my hometown; cards from relatives in Massachusetts and California; rose petals sent from a sacred garden in Guatemala, where apparently "the devout Sisters actually kicked the sarcophagus of the local saint, 'Despertate! Despertate!' [Wake up and *do* something!]"; a bracelet, given to me by Nancy and touched by the Dalai Lama. I want to harness the muscle memory of a body floating above itself, instead of grimaces and spasms, sores and bruises, Lumbar taps and subclavical feeding tubes. If a soul is separate from a body, how does it know to find its way back if not through some invisible magnet that links the head and the heart? A lesson in metaphysics, worthy of any poet:

All this time I have been wondering
if my eyelashes have learned how to sing.

If the climax of the story is the induced deep coma, then the medical antagonists turn into heroes. The technical explanation goes something like this: electrical silence quiets the brain so it can take care of healing. "We were called when they brought you out of the coma," Uncle Dana told me. "Such relief we felt—we started referring to you as a miracle!" A page from September 8th is the last report included in the manila envelope of hospital papers. It chronicles an abnormal EEG due to moderate and marked generalized slowing. No seizures. It's unclear whether this is the deep coma, the lead up to it, or the after effects. Three undocumented weeks lapse.

The summer of no memory culminates with a discharge summary dated September 21, which recaps the Yale months and the history of present illness, reiterates that I was initially admitted with "progressive dementia and psychosis" and tentatively confirms "presumed viral encephalopathy." The abridged version of the hospital narrative uses a fair amount of jargon including *extreme tachycardia* and *episodes of autonomic storms* and even lovelier phrases like *phenobarb coma* and *severe diffuse bilateral slowing*. There are at least two typos on the dot-matrix printed pages. Five hole-punch marks look like waning crescents of the moon lined up against the left margin. Pages are probably missing. The transcription record shows only initials, while the dictating doctor reported on that day that "the patient is currently alert, awake, tracks, attempts to vocalize, will say words and even the correct names of individuals in the room, will, however, not follow commands and will not say more than one word together in any meaningful way." Long term rehabilitation was recommended in flat and unremarkable prose.

As if giving a falling object over to gravity, they discharged me. The orbit had been completed, the patient returned to earth. But reentry landed her in the cloudy stratosphere and then the icy crash of Atlantic waters. And this was only a partial denouement; an end of only one chapter. Transferred to Gaylord Rehabilitation Hospital, I began to put more than one word together in meaningful ways. Memory returned slowly, or rather awareness began to etch itself into the permanence of memory. The summer of no memory was secured into *past,* into *over,* into *finished. Forward* began. But learning to live with the new role as a nineteen-year-old female in long-term rehabilitation meant loss of a different kind. Relearning is a kind of forgetting, after all.

I don't know when I began to get well. As a comet propels through the invisible ellipse, closer and closer to the sun, the cloudy halo that rings the icy nucleus begins to burn up. Blown by solar winds, the coma's fuzzy granules and evaporating ice extend as a long tail of ions and dust across the sky. Evaporation lasted another three months. Waking up took as long as sleeping.

If memory solidifies what we know about ourselves and confirms the story of how we know ourselves, which version of myself can I get back to?

So instead of returning to college, I was given my own room at Gaylord; instead of going home, home came to me. Like an accordion squeezed in and out of the player's hands, I seemed to career through every life stage, contract a little, expand again. First infancy (recognizing faces and voices), then childhood (learning to smile, toilet training, and throwing tantrums), adolescence (laughing about phoniness, drooling over T.V. stars, and fixating on hair and acne), into eventually, adulthood (rediscovering coffee and the power of art). Counting calendar days, waking seemed slow because, like the coma, I couldn't grab onto any of it. There was no exactness, no precision. For others, this pace was a gift, a miracle. Everything seemed amazing when none of it was expected, after a prognosis of maybes and *we'll have to wait and see.* Toddlers don't remember their first steps. Good thing too; otherwise falling would imprint too deeply, and nobody would get up again. I still don't fully understand what it means to come out of nothing, since I can't remember what *nothing* was like.

There would be new storytellers to keep track of waking up—Dad's amateur Polaroids. Maybe photographs suggest false memories, and it's hard to say how much of their input is repair, reinvention or recalculation. My father's black marker didn't start recording the dates until late December, so memory aligns with the pen, not the lens. I remember the camera existed; I remember holding the white tabbed squares as they left its boxy mouth. I don't remember stretching my mouth into an awkward, square grin. I don't remember hugs or conversations or what kind of food we ate when we sat—Shelly, Michael, Kris, and Erick—at a cafeteria table. In these snapshots, everyone looked normal, or what accounts for normal in a photo taken by a camera meant to measure a scene in instants. Maybe that's the key: memory relies on the moment, not the long haul. A photo can hold an instant; a brain smudges it across space and time.

The images still frighten me. My face was a mess; hair cropped short, puffed up without styling, ragged, like I just woke up. My eyes seemed empty but weirdly wild. My expression was amplified, aware the camera was pointed at me. All the pictures show the same face, forced into a smile, pretending excitement yet self-consciously posed.

I had no explanation for my life at Gaylord Hospital, but it seemed like I did not need one. The nurses, therapists, and patients at the hospital were people in my world; they seemed familiar once I started recognizing things. When friends or family visited, they brought presents to my room, talked with me in the upholstered lobby, joined me for dinner. Some afternoons, they'd sit with me outside on the grounds. Thanksgiving night my friend Amanda, driving back from her own celebrations, asked her parents to stop and see me. They walked in "armed with left-over apple pie," as I rested on my bed, quiet but not asleep. She recalled that I sat up, "ramrod and startlingly straight, and gave each one of us a pensive, analyzing stare." Then I looked directly at Amanda's dad, said "Happy Thanksgiving, Spencer," and laid back down.

About this time, others recall too, I started to become more animated, though still not able to fend for myself. I had to relearn how to hold a pencil, how to use the bathroom, how to walk a thousand feet without help. Some days I would be able to shower and dress myself; other days brought pouting, panic, or rage. Frustrations mounted when couldn't articulate my struggle.

Shelly visited me one day during physical therapy; throwing the ball was a big deal at this point. I seem to be over-compensating and trying to make other people feel like I was doing great, very self-conscious. She remembers that I was upset about how I looked, especially the acne. Erick told me about another time when he walked through the hallway with its paneled walls and patterned carpet now familiar to him. He turned the corner and saw me sitting outside my room. My breasts spilled out of whatever shirt I wore, and apparently, I sat there absent-mindedly fondling myself in the hospital chair. Erick felt embarrassment, stood awkwardly, unsure what to do with his sister and the "sweet curiosity" with which she touched herself. A child, hands-on.

More Polaroids pinpoint Christmas, and I think I remember it was a big deal, a special occasion. In one photo—the only one Dad labeled "12/25," Shelly stood next to me outside the hospital doors. My sister was stylish and poised in a dark coat. I dressed like an Arctic explorer, a bluish windbreaker, winter headband. But Shelly wondered if I went home at all on Christmas day. In her memory, the family visited on the 24th, leaving around twilight. From the highway, they passed the mall and Kris commented about not having any presents. Michael remembered picking me up the next morning.

I don't remember dinner or music or if the tree was decorated. I don't remember opening gifts, though a photo labeled vaguely "Xmas" shows me peeling away wrapping from a cylindrical package. I squinted above a graceless smile, maybe wearing lipstick. My cheeks were rosy either from acne scars or from dress-up blush as I showed off new tops—a black and yellow pull-over, another with stripes and a hoodie. I remember the floral dress, silky with scoop neck and fitted sleeves that my sister picked out, but only because I wore it later when clothes began to matter again. Erick stood next to me in one photo, also dressed up in a blue shirt and black tie. In another, Kris wore a Giants tee-shirt; Michael played with the cat. In three or four of these holiday shots, our mother's stencils were visible on the wall behind us as we sat on the couch, like Christmases past. Usually on the other side of the camera, Dad appeared only in one taken at our house; he wore a red sweater and

a look that hinted at relief. I found a thank you note
squeezed into plastic pages of a tiny photo album:

> Dear Dad, Thank you for the pjs. The night-
> gown and the flannel pajamas are pretty. also
> thank you for the socks. I like the junior mints,
> + the Andes candies. lastly, thank you for the
> magazines. Love, Amy

The end of the year was documented by a handful
of photos. On December 29th, everyone came to visit
me at Gaylord for a Christmas party. Dad looked
happy. The new year pictures, pen-marked January
2nd, January 3rd, January 7th showed both home and
hospital, friends visiting, their high school smiles
reassuring me. In one posed shot, I gazed down,
out of focus; my friends were gorgeous and young
and full of life. In another, we ate pizza and drank
Pepsi. I stood in the center wearing a red top and
white leggings. I hunched my shoulders and they
guarded me. I was the only one who looked like she
was faking it. As Amanda described later,

The smiles on our faces betrayed the stark contrasts of our realities. It was a confusing time for those of us with healthy bodies and clear minds. It was clearly beyond our adolescent capabilities to fully grasp the situation.

Their generous familiarity, so necessary when nothing made sense, confirmed the end of ice and darkness. This is when the waking begins and the summer really ends. I turned twenty on January 15th. A month later I started writing.

The journal was a gift, probably a birthday present: glossy, pillowy to the touch, marbled pinks and blues dripped over the cover, the serenity prayer framed in the center. I re-wrote it on the second page, practicing my newly discovered printing techniques. Hand drawn, geometric tulips and bulbous hearts take up another frame on the first page. I wrote the date—my birthday—on the top of the next page. A child's note composed to a child:

hello, Amy I LOVE
poetry I love
once up time
there was a little
elf named Harry
He is a cute elf
I like him the best.

Heart, diamond, full moon, star—four figures, like
suits of a new deck of cards, were drawn below the
scribbled note, above the figure of a train, above
three nearly identical stick figures wearing hats,
the brims connected in one straight line, almost
perfectly parallel to one unified arm stretched across
two shared hands. Greater than, less than, left to
right, their hands reach to the edge of the page.

The next page had five lines: "today is the first day
of your life with love and compassion you will flour-
ish." Then three repeated r's, two crossed out. Below
these was an image that can only be described as an
hourglass—a giant X, bound by two straight lines.
In the geometry of the journal, I drew a playground
of intersecting lines and retraced parallel ones. This
diary lasted for only two entries.

Beginning on February 4, I started a new journal. This one was black covered, 140-sheets, 3-subject notebook, college-ruled, spiral bound—just like the one from college. I kept this one until August, when I would begin another. No other summers would be lost.

> Today was a very special day. I will recap yesterday's happenings. I was expecting my cousin Nancy to arrive via New York City from California at 9:30 a.m. But when she didn't come then, I was a bit upset. Yesturday [sic] morning was not the best.

In my college notes, I focused on the art of reflection; after the illness, I wanted mainly to observe. I wrote every day while at Gaylord, using the journal to keep track of my days, for memory therapy. As I slowly regained connections, there were still little things about my reshaping personality that could not be accounted for. This new self was easily frustrated, which played itself out in many forms. I wrote about feeling normal then having an unexplained "fit" of tears. I threw tantrums in occupational therapy over simple math problems or word games. I would cry, sulk, refuse to go further. My therapist would be forceful with me. I would give up, retreat to my room, then later write a letter of apology.

The early entries recorded small happenings, day-to-day life in rehabilitation. Visitors arrived and left. I wrote about daytrips with the group—mostly to movies ("the theater was big and bright"); outings with family ("brothers came today bearing pizza from Pops. Very good, very nice"); television shows—basketball and game shows; therapy sessions, showers, and "waking up grumpy" or "not much to report, except that we are having a snowstorm." Valentine's day, Holden Caufield, *60 Minutes*. I didn't record everything, keeping tabs on my feelings in limited ways. Monotony was the only structure. I misdated the entries, and so February repeats, but it was really March. A few times I caught myself, crossed out "Feb.," occasionally followed by "did it again." Then the error was duplicated, so I reinvented time: "Feb. 11th Thursday March." The day I moved from the main hospital across the street to Traurig House, the transitional living facility, was recorded as February 16th But "the Big Day" was actually March 16. The next day was St. Patrick's Day.

I spent almost four months in Traurig, building independence, transitioning back to normalcy. A girl named Michelle became my roommate; I volunteered a few hours at the library and renewed my driver's license. Therapies continued at the hospital and later I would follow up as an outpatient. I went home for good on July 3rd.

These are the things I still remember about my time at Gaylord. I still remember John who wore a mustache and had dark brown eyes; he was my first new friend. I still remember the names and faces of therapists, nurses, and orderlies. I remember painting flowers, loving the certainty of stems and petals that were easy to create with flat brushes, uniform brushstrokes, and color. I remember being asked to list animals whose names started with the letter M, but I don't remember whether mouse or monkey was on that list. I remember being told sequences of numbers, never getting past the first four or five, losing them in mid-thought. I remember a pill box with a red plastic top. I remember a boy from group therapy with a traumatic brain injury who wore a steel halo and pins that held his brain in place. I remember being embarrassed for him, and I remember knowing that his TBI was different from my TBI. He had a twisted motorcycle; I had two forgotten seasons. And I still remember the final trip home, a cake decorated with blue and yellow icing waiting for me.

What did I *know*, what do I *remember*, what can I *recall*? Can I pinpoint the month, the day, the core moment, or only the concentric circles that radiate patiently, preserved in pictures? What have I *retained*, and what have I *recreated*? If memory can be sharpened after the fact, if an episode has only to be enhanced, what, then, is real? What is the true story? Once words come back to me, I sense that these too fail without metaphor, without a pen or a gyroscope.

For a long time, I put that half-year away. Mapped in invisible ink, the secret short cut to present tense does not show up, even in the ultraviolet light of memory. Drafts and redrafts skip over the recovery roadblocks of embarrassment and easy silence. I didn't like talking about it anyway. When life goes on, the old script folds faultlessly, slipped into a box in the closet, easily moved across state lines, untraceable in the memory palace. To say it was forgotten would be to say that I remembered it, and no one would want to revisit neuropsychological tests that measure cognition on a sliding scale somewhere between Goethe and Rorschach. No one wants to think she will never be the same.

Memory is a thing; remembering is an action, ongoing. We pause and reflect, let scenes take shape, then relive them. As I grow older, I find myself caught between two territories: loss of memory and loss of memories. Not just the expected losses that come with age, as experience and information accumulate—too much to fit into the webbing of a three-pound brain. But the real losses—my mother's voice, the house on Walker Hill, the dog we had for a few months when I was twelve. Or was I ten? And the fear of irreparable neurological damage. On the other side is the requisite removal of events that signal horror, violence, regret, sadness, anxiety. Forgetting *is* loss—necessary, patient, forgiving. The paradox, though, connects us to the past, to family, to love, stability, and goodness.

Does memory protect us from trauma or does trauma erase memory? A harsh fate or a merciful one? From these collections of images and events—from their scrutiny or oblivion—we splice together the story of our lives. We want the most precious events to be stitched into permanence, and we want the horrors to rocket to the far away dark of space. I remember bandstands in Massachusetts and the fusion of family reunions. I remember long car rides to South Carolina beaches where my brothers played in the loose surf. I remember listening to *Teddy Bear's Picnic* as my sister and I lay in our unpolished brass beds; her blanket was pink-patterned, mine was yellow. I remember watching her bike spin down the dirt road, crashing before I could catch up. I remember the blue shirt my mother wore months into chemotherapy when she showed us her new wig, and I remember the weight of my father's ashes when I carried them home.

Many years later, I ask those close to me to recount their earliest memories. One friend recalls his father's wrath; one still feels the too-tight swaddle of a blanket; another feels the shock of untamed voltage from a wall socket which he childishly poked with a screwdriver. In my earliest memory, I hold a telephone to my ear as my mother reports the birth of my brother Kris. I imagine the greenish Formica tiles of the kitchen and intuit the placement of the refrigerator and stove. It is August. There are curtains on the window. I hang onto the door frame. So many summers later all the objects, colors, and visual clues must be recreated. I don't *remember* these tactile spaces, of course. I can no longer kinesthetically feel my three-and-a-half-year-old body. But these particulars do not diminish the sensation that I associate with this image. Instead of trauma, confinement, or physical shock, this memory points straight to love, to the story of new life, a bigger family, a universe expanding past the circumference of a young girl's tiny brain.

Storylines, like egg-shaped orbits, wobble into themselves. Gravity twists the arc, and resolutions are off-center. I still remember springtime in the rehab house, standing at the countertop, pouring an ordinary cup of coffee, thinking, *this is the way I like coffee*. I still remember the next autumn when I earned an A- in Astronomy 101.

About the Author

Amy Nawrocki is a poet and professor at the University of Bridgeport. She is the author of five collections of poetry and three books of non-fiction, including *Four Blue Eggs, Reconnaissance,* and *Literary Connecticut.* She spent over a year enduring and recovering from a life-threatening encephalitic coma.

visit her at www.amynawrocki.org

LITTLe
BOUND BOOKS
SMALL BOOKS, BIG IMPACT

The Little Bound Books Essay Series
Personal. Poignant. Powerful.

WWW.HOMEBOUNDPUBLICATIONS.COM

**HOMEBOUND
PUBLICATIONS**

Ensuring that the mainstream isn't the only stream.

At Homebound Publications, we publish books written by independent voices for independent minds. Our books focus on a return to simplicity and balance, connection to the earth and each other, and the search for meaning and authenticity. Founded in 2011, Homebound Publications is one of the rising independent publishers in the country. Collectively through our imprints, we publish between fifteen to twenty offerings each year. Our authors have received dozens of awards, including: *Foreword Reviews'* Book of the Year, Nautilus Book Award, Benjamin Franklin Book Awards, and Saltire Literary Awards. Highly-respected among bookstores, readers and authors alike, Homebound Publications has a proven devotion to quality, originality and integrity.

We are a small press with big ideas. As an independent publisher we strive to ensure that the mainstream is not the only stream. It is our intention at Homebound Publications to preserve contemplative storytelling. We publish full-length introspective works of creative non-fiction as well as essay collections, travel writing, poetry, and novels. In all our titles, our intention is to introduce new perspectives that will directly aid humankind in the trials we face at present as a global village.